PIANO SOLO

JAZZ PIANO
Solos

BY JACK REILLY

Photo of Jack Reilly © 2008 by Mike Napoli

ISBN 978-0-7935-6844-4

7777 W. BLUEMOUND RD. P.O. BOX 13819 MILWAUKEE, WI 53213

Visit Hal Leonard Online at
www.halleonard.com

CONTENTS

BIOGRAPHY

Pianist, composer and author Jack Reilly (b. 1932) has the unenviable position of being an artist well respected and admired by his peers for his composing and performing faculties, but never quite achieving that level of public acclaim his prodigious talents deserve.

There was no one defining moment when the pianist decided jazz was to be his livelihood. It grew on him as he hung out at community jazz joints on Staten Island listening to the local piano players. He was pushed over the edge when he heard the modernism of the Lennie Tristano Quintet and made his musical debut with John LaPorta in 1958 at the Newport Jazz Festival. Over the years, he has worked with Ben Webster and with the George Russell Big Band.

Reilly has an impressive musical education resume. In addition to private studies with the aforementioned jazz legend Lennie Tristano, Reilly also studied with the shadowy but influential Hall Overton and composer of contemporary music Ludmila Ulehla. He graduated from the Manhattan School of Music and has been on the faculties of Berklee College of Music and Mannes in New York. He chaired the Jazz Studies Department at the New England Conservatory.

It is this background that compelled Reilly's attention to the instrument. With his exceptional technical skills and musical sensitivity, he could have stuck to the tried-and-true form of standard jazz and pop repertoire. Rather, he took the high-risk but rewarding road of playing his own compositions which are vignettes of modern jazz.

His highly engaging compositions can be heard to best advantage on *The Brinksman*, with a stunning *Masks*, and two masterful albums *Tzu-Jan: The Sound of the Tarot, Vol. 1* and a second volume covering the same theme. These extraordinary recordings provide an impressionist avocation of the exotic Thoth Tarot Cards.

—**David Nathan.**

COMPOSITIONS

JACK REILLY'S COMPOSITIONS INCLUDE:

Orbitals - Concerto for jazz piano trio and symphony orchestra; in one movement
Duration 35 minutes

A Jazz Requiem - for jazz quintet, jazz vocal soloist and 62-voice mixed chorus
Duration 62 minutes

The Light of the Soul - Oratorio for narrator, 10-piece jazz ensemble, mixed choir and vocal soloists;
based on the Yoga Sutras of Patanjali
Duration 71 Minutes

Chuang-Tzu - Theme and 8 variations for symphony orchestra
Duration 26 minutes

Seventeen Lullabys for Orchestra
Duration 35 minutes

Concertino or Solo Jazz Piano (trio optional) - with string orchestra
Duration 35 minutes

Concerto for Chromatic Harmonica and Strings
Duration 26 Minutes

The Silence of the One - 24 piano pieces, in all 24 keys;
Books One and Two, for solo piano (trio optional)
Duration 2 hours

Being and Time [in progress] - for narrator, two pianos, jazz quartet, soprano and baritone vocal soloists,
and 125-voice mixed choir
Duration (will be) approx. 2 hours

*"Jack Reilly's music is singular, almost private, and yet it reaches beyond his personal vision.
This is music that speaks to the collective spirit of mankind."*
—Bill Charlap

"Jack, your music and playing takes Jazz to a new level."
—Dave Brubeck (on hearing Jack's recording, *Masks*).

*"One of our great contemporary acoustic pianists... a singular intelligence
of remarkable purity and consistency."*
—Chuck Berg, *Jazz Times*

ALL THE THINGS YOU ARE

from VERY WARM FOR MAY
[Version 1]

Lyrics by OSCAR HAMMERSTEIN II
Music by JEROME KERN

ALL THE THINGS YOU ARE

from VERY WARM FOR MAY

[Version 2]

Lyrics by OSCAR HAMMERSTEIN II
Music by JEROME KERN

AUTUMN SUITE

I. Waltz for Fall

Composed by
JACK REILLY

Flowing

II. Halloween

Composed by
JACK REILLY

Easy Swing

III. November

Composed by
JACK REILLY

Moderately

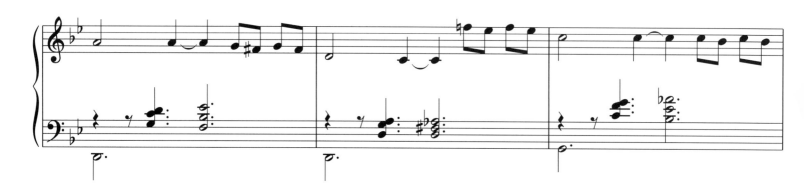

Dedicated to Claire Lian

CLARA'S BELL

Composed by JACK REILLY

BODY AND SOUL

Words by EDWARD HEYMAN,
ROBERT SOUR and FRANK EYTON
Music by JOHN GREEN

Expressively

HERE'S THAT RAINY DAY

Words by JOHNNY BURKE
Music by JIMMY VAN HEUSEN

Slowly

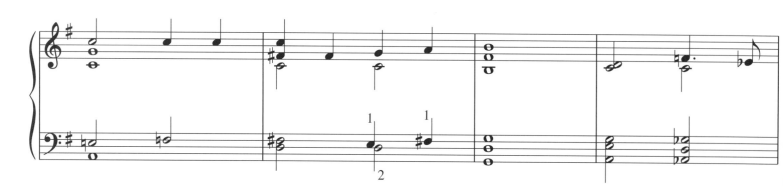

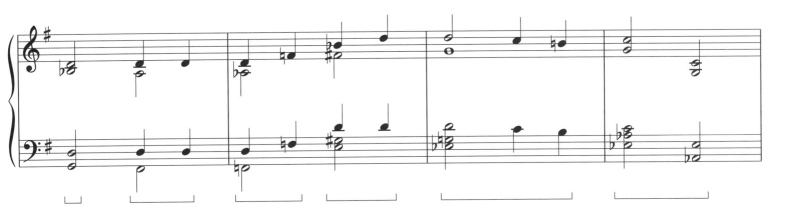

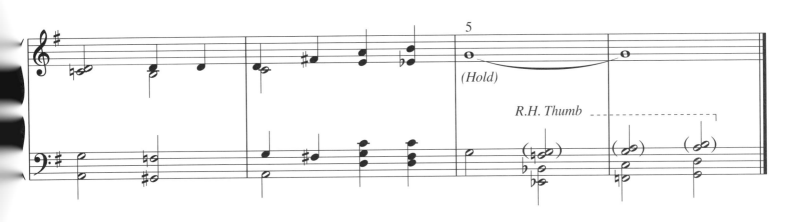

I CAN'T GET STARTED WITH YOU

Words by IRA GERSHWIN
Music by VERNON DUKE

Slowly

I CONCENTRATE ON YOU

Words and Music by
COLE PORTER

Moderately

I COULD WRITE A BOOK

Words by LORENZ HART
Music by RICHARD RODGERS

Moderately

I THOUGHT ABOUT YOU

Words by JOHNNY MERCER
Music by JIMMY VAN HEUSEN

Slowly

MY SHINING HOUR
from the Motion Picture THE SKY'S THE LIMIT

Lyric by JOHNNY MERCER
Music by HAROLD ARLEN

Moderately

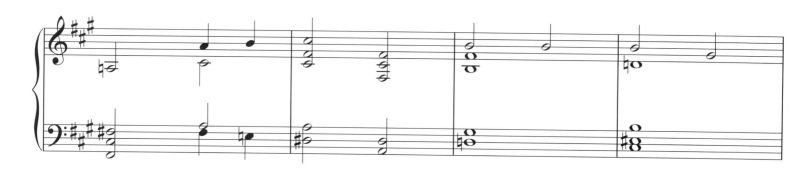

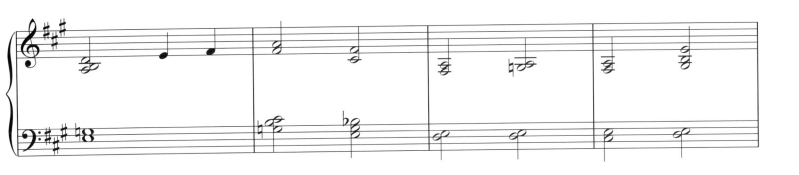

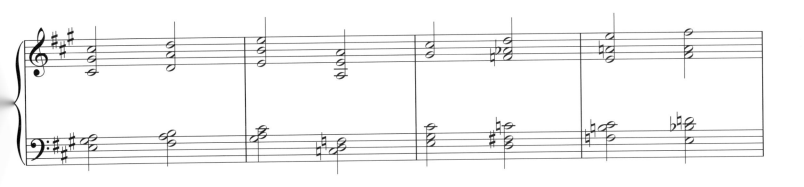

RAINDROPS KEEP FALLIN'
ON MY HEAD

Lyric by HAL DAVID
Music by BURT BACHARACH

Rhythmically

RUBY, MY DEAR

By THELONIOUS MONK

Moderately

SPRING CAN REALLY
HANG YOU UP THE MOST

Lyric by FRAN LANDESMAN
Music by TOMMY WOLF

Slowly

TENDERLY

Lyric by JACK LAWRENCE
Music by WALTER GROSS

Slowly

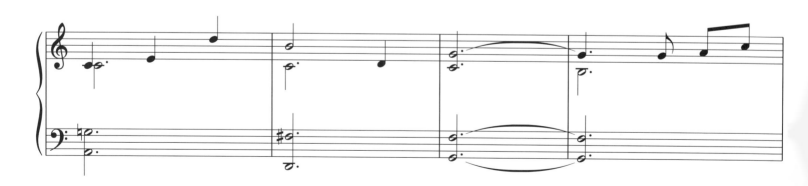

  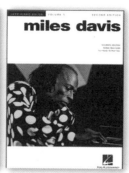   

INCLUDES CHORD NAMES!

jazz piano solos series

Each volume features exciting new arrangements of the songs which helped define a style.

vol. 1 miles davis - second edition
New piano solo arrangements of 19 classic tunes by the great Miles Davis: All Blues • Blue in Green • Boplicity (Be Bop Lives) • Circle • Dig • Eighty One • Four • Freddie Freeloader • Half Nelson • Miles • Milestones • Nardis • So What • Solar • Somethin' Else • Tune Up • and more.
00306521 Piano Solo.................................. $14.95

vol. 2 jazz blues - second edition
This collection presents 26 jazz-blues classics served up for solo piano. Songs: All Blues • Au Privave • Birk's Works • Blue Monk • Blues in the Closet • C-Jam Blues • Freddie Freeloader • Mr. P.C. • Now's the Time • Straight No Chaser • and more.
00306522 Piano Solo.................................. $14.99

vol. 3 latin jazz
17 Latin jazz classics, including: Brazil (Xavier Cugat, Django Reinhardt) • Manteca (Dizzy Gillespie, Cal Tjader) • Mas Que Nada (Dizzy Gillespie) • Perfidia (Perez Prado, Nat King Cole) • Triste (Antonio Carlos Jobim, Cal Tjader) • and more.
00310621 Piano Solo.................................. $14.99

vol. 4 bebop jazz
25 classics from jazz masters of the '40s and '50s, such as Charlie Parker, Dizzy Gillespie, Thelonious Monk, Sonny Rollins, Ella Fitzgerald and others. Tunes include: Anthropology • Au Privave • Billie's Bounce • Doxy • Half Nelson • In Walked Bud • Lady Bird • Lemon Drop • Well You Needn't • Woodyn' You • and more.
00310709 Piano Solo.................................. $14.95

vol. 5 cool jazz - second edition
23 tunes from the '50s and '60s jazz cats who invented "cool," including: All Blues (Miles Davis, George Benson) • A Ballad (Gerry Mulligan, Stan Getz) • Con Alma (Dizzy Gillespie, Stan Getz) • Epistrophy (Thelonious Monk) • Nardis (Bill Evans, Joe Henderson) • Take Five (Dave Brubeck, George Benson) • and more.
00310710 Piano Solo.................................. $14.99

vol. 6 hard bop
18 jazz classics from the '50s and '60s, including: The Champ (Dizzy Gillespie, Jimmy Smith) • Giant Steps (John Coltrane, Tommy Flanagan) • Mercy, Mercy, Mercy (Cannonball Adderley, Joe Zawinul) • Song for My Father (Kenny Burrell, Horace Silver) • This Here (Bobby Timmons, Cannonball Adderly) • and more.
00310711 Piano Solo.................................. $14.95

vol. 7 smooth jazz
19 contemporary favorites: Cast Your Fate to the Wind (David Benoit) • Just the Two of Us (Grover Washington, Jr.) • Morning Dance (Spyro Gyra) • Mountain Dance (Dave Grusin) • This Masquerade (George Benson) • We're in This Love Together (Al Jarreau) • and more.
00310727 Piano Solo.................................. $14.99

vol. 8 jazz pop
New jazz piano arrangements of 22 classic pop songs, including: Blackbird • Don't Know Why • Fields of Gold • Isn't She Lovely • It's Too Late • New York State of Mind • On Broadway • Oye Como Va • Roxanne • What a Fool Believes • You Are So Beautiful • and more.
00311786 Piano Solo.................................. $14.95

vol. 9 duke ellington
New piano solo arrangements of 24 beloved Duke Ellington songs, including: Caravan • Don't Get Around Much Anymore • It Don't Mean a Thing • Mood Indigo • Satin Doll • Take the "A" Train • and more.
00311787 Piano Solo.................................. $14.99

vol. 10 jazz ballads
Fresh solo piano arrangements of 24 favorite ballads in a jazz style, including: Body and Soul • I Guess I'll Hang My Tears Out to Dry • Misty • My Funny Valentine • The Nearness of You • When I Fall in Love • and more.
00311788 Piano Solo.................................. $14.99

vol. 11 soul jazz
22 tunes full of soul, including: Chitlins Con Carne • Dat Dere • Five Spot After Dark • The "In" Crowd • The Midnight Special • Sister Sadie • Soultrane • Unchain My Heart • What'd I Say • You Are My Sunshine • and more.
00311789 Piano Solo.................................. $14.99

vol. 12 swinging jazz
Hip new piano solo arrangements of 24 swinging classics, including: Ain't That a Kick in the Head • All of Me • Beyond the Sea • Bluesette • Come Fly with Me • It's Only a Paper Moon • Just in Time • Route 66 • Steppin' Out with My Baby • Witchcraft • and more.
00311797 Piano Solo.................................. $14.99

vol. 13 jazz gems
21 jazz classics arranged for solo piano with chord names: All Too Soon • Confirmation • Don't Explain • Line for Lyons • Little Sunflower • Naima (Niema) • A Night in Tunisia • Nuages • Spain • Stablemates • Stolen Moments • Topsy • Two Bass Hit • and more.
00311899 Piano Solo.................................. $14.99

vol. 14 jazz classics
Rich piano solo arrangements with chord names of 21 of the best jazz gems of all time: Bernie's Tune • Birdland • Donna Lee • Footprints • Impressions • On Green Dolphin Street • Red Clay • Robbin's Nest • St. Thomas • Turn Out the Stars • Yardbird Suite • and more.
00311900 Piano Solo.................................. $14.99

vol. 15 bossa nova
Solo arrangements with chord names of 20 swinging Latin standards: Agua De Beber • Call Me • Estate • The Girl from Ipanema • Meditation • Quiet Nights of Quiet Stars • Watch What Happens • Wave • more!
00311906 Piano Solo.................................. $14.99

HAL•LEONARD® CORPORATION
7777 W. BLUEMOUND RD. P.O. BOX 13819 MILWAUKEE, WI 53213

www.halleonard.com